# 365
# Thought-Provoking
# Questions for Girls
# Aged 15-17

# 365 Thought-Provoking Questions for Girls Aged 15-17

## One Question a Day for Personal Growth and Bolstering Identity

Aria Capri Publishing
Devon Abbruzzese
Mauricio Vasquez

Toronto, Canada

<u>Authors:</u>
Devon Abbruzzese
Mauricio Vasquez
Aria Capri Publishing

First Printing: May 2024

ISBN-978-1-998402-46-5 (Paperback book)
ISBN-978-1-998402-45-8 (Hardcover book)
ISBN-978-1-998402-44-1 (Electronic book)

# Introduction

Welcome to a journey of inquiry and insight, tailored specifically for middle adolescent girls navigating the pivotal ages of 15 to 17. This book is dedicated to those who stand on the brink of adulthood, exploring who they are while molding who they will become. Our focus here transcends traditional advice; instead, we delve into the profound impact of engaging in thoughtful questioning to promote personal growth and strengthen relationships.

The Power of Questions

In adolescence, a unique and transformative stage of life, the power of asking the right questions cannot be overstated. Questions are the keys that unlock the mysteries of one's own mind and the world around them. For girls navigating middle adolescence, each question posed in this book serves as a gentle nudge towards self-discovery and empowerment. By exploring these questions, young women can develop a deeper understanding of their values, aspirations, and challenges.

Why Questions Matter

During middle adolescence, girls experience rapid changes—not only physically but also emotionally and socially. They are forming identities, establishing independence, and learning to navigate complex social landscapes. It's a time when relationships, both with peers and adults, gain new depth and significance.

Asking thoughtful, engaging questions does more than just spark conversation. It encourages introspection and self-expression, which are critical for emotional and cognitive development. Thoughtful questions can help adolescents articulate their thoughts and feelings, which is a foundational step towards emotional intelligence.

Building Relationships Through Inquiry

For parents, educators, and mentors, questions are a powerful tool for connecting with adolescent girls. They provide a nonintrusive way to show interest and build trust. When adults ask genuine, open-ended questions, they send a clear message: "Your thoughts matter. Your feelings are important. I am here to listen." This supportive approach fosters stronger relationships and helps adolescents feel valued and understood.

Personal Growth Through Self-Exploration

This book encourages girls to reflect on a wide array of topics—ranging from their aspirations and fears to their beliefs about justice and beauty. Each question is designed to challenge them to think critically and creatively, developing skills that will benefit them throughout their lives. These skills include problem-solving, critical thinking, and empathizing with others.

Transformative Impact

Engaging with these questions can transform how young women perceive themselves and their relationships. It can lead to increased self-awareness, greater resilience, and a more profound understanding of one's own mental and emotional landscape. Moreover, it prepares them to face life's challenges with confidence and curiosity, equipped with a stronger sense of their own identity and values.

A Call to Engage

As you embark on this year-long journey of questions, remember that the process of asking and reflecting is as important as any answer you may discover. This book is not just a guide but a companion in your exploration of the vibrant, tumultuous, and deeply rewarding years of middle adolescence.

We invite you, the reader, to open your mind to the questions within these pages. Let them inspire you, challenge you, and guide you toward a fuller understanding of yourself and your place in the world. For parents and mentors, we hope these questions serve as a bridge, connecting you to the young women in your lives in meaningful and transformative ways.

Let the journey of questions begin.

Devon & Mauricio

# Scan the QR code to access the full collection

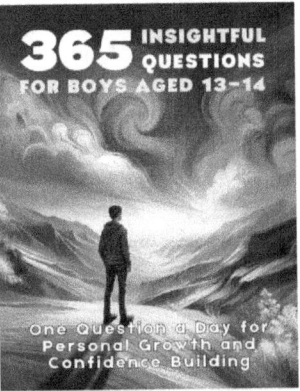

# Guidelines for Asking Questions to Adolescents

Read the following guidelines to learn more about asking questions that unlock learning, foster communication and improve relationships.

- **Effective questions are open or focused, depending on the context**: Questions that open awareness and learning are open-ended questions that cannot be answered with a yes or no. Such questions evoke deeper thinking and reflection.

- **Effective questions support learning**: The goal is to stimulate thinking and deepen understanding of the situation. Insightful questions should focus attention on the most valuable aspects of the issue at hand, helping adolescents understand their experiences and feelings better.

- **Effective questions are asked for the benefit of others**: The intent is to stimulate the thinking and deepen the understanding of adolescents. It is not necessarily about the questioner and their needs.

- **Effective questions engage a personal response**: Engaging adolescents by inviting a personal response—how they feel, what emotions they are bringing to the situation—is crucial. The more a question invites a personal response to a challenge or choice, the more powerful it is for facilitating learning and growth.

- **Effective questions look beyond problems to future outcomes**: When adolescents are entangled in a problem, impactful questions shift the perspective from the problem to the solution, opening new opportunities for action and positive thinking.

- **Effective questions facilitate openness versus defensiveness**: Impactful questions are worded and expressed with a non-judgmental tone and open body language to prevent a defensive reaction. It is usually best to avoid questions that begin with "why" since they often elicit defensive responses or explanations.

- **Effective questions co-create best options versus manipulating outcomes**: Impactful questions are not intended to manipulate or lead adolescents to the option you might think is the best. If you want to suggest, it is best made directly as a suggestion versus a disguised directive through a question.

- **Less is more**: For questions, less is usually more. Ask only one question at a time and avoid long-winded, complicated questions.

## <u>Share Your Experience</u>

Thank you for choosing this book. We hope this has provided meaningful insights and fostered valuable conversations for you and your child.

Your feedback helps us improve and helps other parents and young readers discover this resource. Reviews increase the book's visibility, making it easier for those who might benefit from its content to find it.

If you found this book helpful, please take a moment to leave a review by scanning this QR code.

Your experience can inspire and guide others on their journey of self-discovery and growth. We appreciate your support. Thank you.

Devon & Mauricio

# Disclaimer

Dear Readers,

This book is designed to serve as a tool for personal growth, reflection, and exploring thoughts and feelings. The questions provided within these pages aim to inspire introspection and conversation, fostering a deeper understanding of oneself and the world.

However, it is important to understand that this book is not a substitute for professional advice, diagnosis, or treatment. While the questions can guide meaningful discussions and self-discovery, they are not intended to address or resolve serious issues or health concerns.

If you or your child encounters significant emotional, psychological, or physical challenges, we strongly recommend seeking the guidance of a qualified professional. This may include consulting a doctor, mental health professional, counselor, or any other relevant specialist who can provide the appropriate support and interventions.

The publisher, author, and any associated parties take no responsibility for any consequences resulting from the use of this book. It is up to the reader to exercise their judgment and discretion when engaging with the questions and interpreting their answers. The insights and reflections gained from this book should be seen as a starting point for further exploration and, when necessary, professional consultation.

We hope that this book serves as a valuable resource for personal growth and development. Remember, each individual's journey of self-discovery is unique, and seeking help when needed is a sign of strength and wisdom.

### Day 1

How do you define happiness, and what are three things that make you genuinely happy?

### Day 2

What physical activities do you enjoy the most, and how do they make you feel afterward?

### Day 3

When you face a difficult problem, what is your strategy for solving it?

### Day 4

Have you ever felt misunderstood by your peers or adults? What happened, and how did it make you feel?

### Day 5
How do your cultural values influence the decisions you make in your life?

### Day 6
What are some ways you manage stress when you feel overwhelmed by school or personal issues?

### Day 7
What does a perfect day look like to you, and why?

### Day 8
How do you think your life is different living in an urban or rural setting?

### Day 9
What are three qualities you admire in your closest friends?

### Day 10
How do you think social media influences your perceptions of what a "normal" life should look like?

### Day 11
What subjects in school do you find most challenging, and why do you think that is?

### Day 12
How do you think your understanding of right and wrong has changed as you've gotten older?

## Day 13
What steps do you take to ensure your personal safety when you are out with friends?

## Day 14
How do you feel about your future? What excites or worries you the most about it?

## Day 15
Have you ever helped someone in need? What did you do, and how did it make you feel?

## Day 16
How do you express yourself when you are angry, and what strategies help you calm down?

### Day 17
What role does exercise play in your life? Do you think it affects your mood or concentration?

### Day 18
How has your relationship with your family changed as you have become a teenager?

### Day 19
What are your thoughts on maintaining physical health? How important is it to you?

### Day 20
When was the last time you tried something new, and what did you learn from the experience?

### Day 21

How do you approach conflicts with friends or family? Do you think your strategies are effective?

### Day 22

In what ways do you think being a teenager today is different from when your parents were teens?

### Day 23

What are your favorite ways to relax and unwind after a stressful day?

### Day 24

How do you handle peer pressure when it comes to making decisions that impact your health or morals?

**Day 25**
What does "being successful" mean to you?

**Day 26**
How do you prioritize your tasks for schoolwork or personal projects?

**Day 27**
Have you ever experienced cyberbullying or seen it happen to someone else? How did you react?

**Day 28**
What are some things you feel your community could improve for teenagers?

### Day 29
How do you define a good leader, and do you see yourself as one?

### Day 30
What are your top three goals for this year, and how do you plan to achieve them?

### Day 31
How does your family heritage influence your daily life and values?

### Day 32
What are the most important factors you consider when making decisions about your future?

### Day 33
How do you feel about the environmental challenges our planet faces?

### Day 34
What inspires you to learn and how do you motivate yourself when you're not interested?

### Day 35
How has your perspective on what matters most in friendships changed over the past few years?

### Day 36
What personal achievements are you most proud of, and why?

## Day 37

How do you feel about the changes your body has gone through during puberty?

## Day 38

Can you think of a time when understanding someone else's feelings helped resolve a conflict?

## Day 39

What are your thoughts on the role of technology in education? Has it made learning easier or more complicated for you?

## Day 40

How do you deal with feelings of sadness or disappointment?

### Day 41
What does "family" mean to you, and who do you consider part of your family?

### Day 42
How have your priorities changed in the past year, and what influenced these changes?

### Day 43
Do you feel that your school environment supports your mental health? Why or why not?

### Day 44
What are your strategies for dealing with distractions when you need to focus?

### Day 45
Have you ever had to stand up for someone else? What happened and how did it make you feel?

### Day 46
How does your cultural background influence your friendships?

### Day 47
What kind of role model do you aspire to be for younger kids?

### Day 48
How do you handle criticism from others, particularly on social media?

### Day 49
What are your views on the importance of physical activity in school settings?

### Day 50
How does the media portrayal of women affect your self-image and self-esteem?

### Day 51
When you think about your future career, what are the most important factors you consider?

### Day 52
How do you maintain your emotional well-being during exams or other stressful academic periods?

## Day 53
What aspects of your life do you think most affect your mental health?


## Day 54
How do you balance your personal life with your academic responsibilities?


## Day 55
Can you think of a book or movie that significantly impacted your view of the world? Why did it have such an effect?


## Day 56
What does ethical online behavior mean to you, and how do you practice it?

### Day 57

How do you approach making new friends, and what qualities do you look for in a friend?

### Day 58

Have you ever faced a dilemma where you had to choose between a friend and your morals?

### Day 59

How do you feel about the diversity (or lack thereof) in your school or community?

### Day 60

What is one global issue you are passionate about, and how do you think young people can make a difference?

### Day 61
How do you define personal success, and how do you measure it?

### Day 62
What experiences have taught you the most about yourself?

### Day 63
How does nature or spending time outdoors influence your mood and thoughts?

### Day 64
What traditions from your culture do you find most meaningful?

### Day 65
How do you think mental health awareness can be improved in schools?

### Day 66
What steps do you take to ensure your own safety online?

### Day 67
How do you manage your time between schoolwork and hobbies?

### Day 68
What is one piece of advice you would give to a younger girl about navigating high school?

## Day 69
How do you handle situations where you feel peer pressure to conform to certain behaviors?

## Day 70
What skills do you think are necessary for managing personal finances?

## Day 71
How do you approach learning about new cultures and their practices?

## Day 72
Have you ever volunteered or engaged in community service? What did you learn from the experience?

### Day 73
What are your thoughts on sustainable living, and how do you incorporate sustainability into your life?

### Day 74
How do you prioritize your mental health when faced with academic and social pressures?

### Day 75
How do you reconcile differences in opinion with close friends or family members?

### Day 76
What motivates you to keep going when you encounter obstacles?

### Day 77
How do you express your creativity, and what activities make you feel most creative?

### Day 78
What has been the most challenging aspect of your education, and how have you addressed it?

### Day 79
How do you think travel or exposure to different places can impact a person's worldview?

### Day 80
How does the way you present yourself on social media differ from your real-life personality?

### Day 81
What are the most important lessons you've learned from your parents?

### Day 82
How do you deal with changes, both big and small, in your life?

### Day 83
What role does spirituality or religion play in your life?

### Day 84
How do you think your experiences as a teenager will influence your adult life

## Day 85
What methods do you find most effective for learning new information?

## Day 86
What role does music play in your life, and how does it affect your emotions?

## Day 87
How do you approach making decisions about your health, such as diet and exercise?

## Day 88
What are your strategies for maintaining focus and motivation when studying for difficult subjects?

## Day 89

How do you define a healthy relationship? What qualities make a relationship healthy?

## Day 90

What do you think are the most significant pressures faced by teenagers today?

## Day 91

How do you feel about the portrayal of teenage girls in movies and on television?

## Day 92

In what ways do you think being a teenager in today's world is different from your parents' generation?

## Day 93
How do you deal with the expectations set by your family, school, or society?



## Day 94
What does leadership mean to you, and in what ways are you a leader in your community or school?



## Day 95
How do you handle disagreements with people who have different viewpoints?



## Day 96
What are the benefits and challenges of having a diverse group of friends?

### Day 97

How do you think your experiences during adolescence will shape your future?

### Day 98

What are the most effective ways you have found to deal with anxiety or stress?

### Day 99

How do you manage your responsibilities at home, school, and in your personal life?

### Day 100

What steps do you take to build and maintain your self-esteem?

### Day 101
How does your family celebrate successes or achievements?

### Day 102
What do you find most rewarding about learning new things?

### Day 103
How do you approach problem-solving when faced with a challenge that seems insurmountable?

### Day 104
What impact has social media had on your relationships with peers?

## Day 105
How do you prepare for important discussions or decisions with your parents?

## Day 106
What actions do you take to protect your emotional well-being?

## Day 107
How do you express gratitude in your daily life?

## Day 108
What are your thoughts on gender roles in today's society?

## Day 109
How do you approach conflicts or misunderstandings with your siblings or close friends?

## Day 110
What experiences have influenced your views on money and financial management?

## Day 111
How do you find balance between technology use and other aspects of your life?

## Day 112
What are your thoughts on the importance of community service?

### Day 113
How do you set goals for yourself, and what helps you achieve them?

### Day 114
How do you approach discussions about difficult topics with friends or family?

### Day 115
What are the key factors that influence your clothing and style choices?

### Day 116
How do you feel about the future of the environment, and what role do you see yourself playing in it?

## Day 117
How do you deal with feelings of jealousy or envy?

## Day 118
What do you think is the biggest challenge facing your generation?

## Day 119
How do you nurture your mental health during times of change?

## Day 120
What have you learned about yourself from participating in team sports or group activities?

## Day 121
How do you deal with setbacks or failures?

## Day 122
What does it mean to be a good friend?

## Day 123
How do you prioritize tasks when you have multiple deadlines?

## Day 124
What impact do you want to have on the world?

## Day 125
How do you maintain your physical and mental health during busy times?

## Day 126
What inspires you to keep learning outside of school?

## Day 127
How do you manage your digital footprint and protect your online privacy?

## Day 128
What are your strategies for dealing with procrastination?

## Day 129
How do you develop trust in relationships?

## Day 130
What do you think are the keys to maintaining good mental health?

## Day 131
How do you handle the pressure to conform to societal expectations?

## Day 132
What are your thoughts on the balance between individual freedom and social responsibility?

### Day 133
How do you cope with the uncertainty about what you want to do in the future?

### Day 134
How do you decide whom to trust with personal problems or challenges?

### Day 135
What strategies do you use to enhance your creativity and problem-solving skills?

### Day 136
What personal values are most important to you, and how do they guide your decisions?

### Day 137
How do you recognize when someone is a positive influence in your life?

### Day 138
What methods do you use to calm yourself when you feel overwhelmed by emotions?

### Day 139
How has your perspective on the world changed in the last year?

### Day 140
What are the top three things you feel you contribute to your friendships?

## Day 141
How do you think your education has shaped your views on the world?

## Day 142
What steps do you take when you feel excluded or left out by your peers?

## Day 143
How do you determine if a source of information is trustworthy, especially on the internet?

## Day 144
In what ways do you think traveling or living in different places can influence a person's character or beliefs?

## Day 145
How do you approach discussions about sensitive or controversial topics?

## Day 146
What has been your most empowering moment and why?

## Day 147
How do you go about setting and maintaining boundaries in your personal and digital interactions?

## Day 148
What do you think is the role of art or creativity in personal development?

## Day 149
How do you deal with the pressure to succeed academically or in extracurricular activities?

## Day 150
What are some ways you can help promote equality and fairness in your community?

## Day 151
How do you decide what personal information to share on social media?

## Day 152
What inspires you to change something in your community or school?

### Day 153
How do you handle moments when you feel misunderstood by adults?

### Day 154
What activities help you reconnect with yourself when you feel lost or uncertain?

### Day 155
How do you evaluate your own progress or success in personal goals?

### Day 156
What role does forgiveness play in your relationships?

## Day 157
How do you encourage yourself to try new things, even when you're nervous or unsure?

## Day 158
What has been the biggest challenge in maintaining your physical health?

## Day 159
How do you think modern technology will shape the future of your career or life?

## Day 160
What qualities do you think are essential for a leader to possess?

### Day 161
How do you handle feelings of competitiveness with your peers?

### Day 162
What are your thoughts on the importance of privacy in today's digital age?

### Day 163
How do you find support when you feel isolated from your peers or community?

### Day 164
What has been a significant change in your life recently, and how have you adapted to it?

## Day 165
How do you think personal challenges have shaped your identity?

## Day 166
What practices do you find most effective for maintaining mental clarity and focus?

## Day 167
How do you approach learning from your mistakes?

## Day 168
What does 'being healthy' mean to you, and how do you pursue health in your daily life?

## Day 169
How do you balance your own needs with the needs of others around you?

## Day 170
What steps do you take to cultivate a positive self-image?

## Day 171
How do you approach resolving conflicts with someone who has a different perspective than yours?

## Day 172
What are some creative ways you express yourself?

### Day 173
How do you maintain motivation for schoolwork during periods of low interest or fatigue?

### Day 174
What are your strategies for building resilience in the face of adversity?

### Day 175
How do you feel about taking risks, and can you share a time when taking a risk led to a positive outcome?

### Day 176
How has your understanding of friendship evolved over the years?

### Day 177

What are some ways you contribute to making your school or community a better place?

### Day 178

How do you deal with expectations from yourself and others to perform well in every aspect of your life?

### Day 179

What are the most effective ways you've found to manage time between school, hobbies, and social activities?

### Day 180

How do you define success in personal relationships?

### Day 181
How do you feel about the future of your community and your role in it?

### Day 182
What experiences have significantly shaped your views on love and relationships?

### Day 183
How do you prioritize your mental and physical health during busy times?

### Day 184
What lessons have you learned about teamwork from group projects or sports?

### Day 185

How do you determine which of your traits are strengths and which are areas for improvement?

### Day 186

How do you respond when you encounter failure, and what do you learn from these experiences?

### Day 187

What changes would you like to see in your school environment, and how can you contribute to making them happen?

### Day 188

How do you define courage, and can you share a time when you had to be courageous?

### Day 189

What are the most important factors you consider when planning for your future career?

### Day 190

How do you manage your emotional reactions during heated discussions?

### Day 191

What inspires you to keep pursuing your hobbies or interests?

### Day 192

How do you stay informed about current events, and why do you think it's important?

## Day 193

What are the benefits of having a diverse set of friends, and how do these relationships affect your worldview?

## Day 194

How do you ensure you are respecting others' boundaries, and how do you communicate your own?

## Day 195

What are your strategies for overcoming self-doubt?

## Day 196

How do you maintain a balance between digital connectivity and real-life interactions?

## Day 197
Can you describe a time when you had to advocate for yourself or others?

## Day 198
What role does empathy play in your relationships?

## Day 199
How do you approach the challenge of balancing school obligations with personal life?

## Day 200
What aspects of your culture do you celebrate, and how do they enrich your life?

### Day 201

How do you handle the pressures of social expectations regarding appearance and behavior?

### Day 202

What strategies do you use to build new friendships while maintaining old ones?

### Day 203

How do you assess risks and benefits when making important decisions?

### Day 204

What are your thoughts on the role of discipline in achieving goals?

## Day 205

How do you approach dealing with change, particularly changes that are outside of your control?

## Day 206

What steps do you take to stay safe when using the internet?

## Day 207

How do you handle conflicts that arise within your friend group?

## Day 208

What does "mental wellness" mean to you, and how do you practice it?

## Day 209
How do you decide when to follow your heart versus when to follow your head?

## Day 210
How has your understanding of what it means to be healthy evolved?

## Day 211
What are your thoughts on the importance of self-care, and what are your favorite self-care activities?

## Day 212
How do you deal with the stress of uncertainty about the future?

### Day 213
What role do you think forgiveness plays in personal growth?

### Day 214
How do you determine if you are spending too much time on digital devices?

### Day 215
How do you stay motivated when you don't see immediate results from your efforts?

### Day 216
What has been your experience with teamwork in sports, school projects, or other activities?

### Day 217
How do you approach learning about viewpoints different from your own?

### Day 218
What are the key characteristics that make a leader effective in your eyes?

### Day 219
How do you prioritize which social issues are most important to you?

### Day 220
What are some ways you've found effective for managing your time efficiently?

### Day 221
How do you navigate the balance between maintaining privacy and sharing your life on social media?

### Day 222
What are the biggest challenges you face when trying to maintain physical fitness?

### Day 223
How do you determine the credibility of information you find online?

### Day 224
What has been the most impactful advice you've ever received, and why?

### Day 225
How do you approach conversations about sensitive or difficult topics with your parents or guardians?

### Day 226
What are the qualities you value most in a teacher or mentor?

### Day 227
How do you define personal integrity, and how do you strive to uphold it?

### Day 228
What are your thoughts on the importance of artistic expression?

## Day 229
How do you balance your aspirations with your current responsibilities?

## Day 230
What actions do you take to conserve the environment in your daily life?

## Day 231
How do you cope with peer pressure when it conflicts with your values?

## Day 232
What are your strategies for handling disappointment or setbacks?

## Day 233
How do you define a successful life?

## Day 234
What steps do you take to prepare for important exams or projects?

## Day 235
How has your relationship with your siblings or close relatives shaped who you are today?

## Day 236
What does it mean to you to be a good citizen in your community?

### Day 237
How do you deal with the influence of peer pressure when it comes to making ethical decisions?

### Day 238
Can you share a moment when you felt a strong sense of accomplishment? What led to it?

### Day 239
How do you approach setting personal boundaries in relationships?

### Day 240
What activities help you manage stress most effectively?

### Day 241
How do you nurture your creative talents, and why is creativity important to you?

### Day 242
What is the most challenging aspect of your education so far, and how are you addressing it?

### Day 243
How do you handle situations where you have to work with someone who has a very different approach or attitude?

### Day 244
What are the most valuable lessons you have learned from a difficult experience?

### Day 245
How do you think self-awareness contributes to personal growth?

### Day 246
What are your strategies for staying engaged in subjects that do not immediately interest you?

### Day 247
How do you balance the desire for independence with family expectations?

### Day 248
What role do hobbies play in your life, and how do they influence your wellbeing?

### Day 249
How do you define and pursue happiness in your daily life?

### Day 250
What steps do you take to build confidence in areas where you feel uncertain?

### Day 251
How do you deal with feelings of insecurity or comparison with others?

### Day 252
What are the key ways you contribute to a positive environment at school?

## Day 253
How do you approach problem-solving in unexpected situations?

## Day 254
What role does gratitude play in your life, and how do you express it?

## Day 255
How do you maintain motivation for personal goals when progress seems slow?

## Day 256
How do you manage the balance between schoolwork and spending time with friends and family?

### Day 257

What are your thoughts on the role of mentorship in personal and professional development?

### Day 258

How do you respond to changes in friendships as you and your peers grow and evolve?

### Day 259

What has been your most meaningful travel experience, and why?

### Day 260

How do you prioritize your commitments to make the best use of your time?

### Day 261
What are your strategies for dealing with the fear of failure?

### Day 262
How do you maintain your mental health when faced with ongoing academic pressure?

### Day 263
How do you approach conflicts in a way that leads to constructive solutions?

### Day 264
What does it mean to you to be a supportive friend?

## Day 265
How do you think about and plan for your financial future?



## Day 266
What are the key factors that help you make informed decisions?



## Day 267
How do you handle situations where you need to stand up for your beliefs?



## Day 268
What personal achievements in the last year are you most proud of?

## Day 269
How do you cultivate resilience in times of personal challenge?

## Day 270
What does leadership look like to you in everyday situations?

## Day 271
How do you encourage yourself to stay positive during tough times?

## Day 272
What role does reflection play in your personal development?

### Day 273
How do you determine which relationships are most valuable and nurturing for you?

### Day 274
What impact do you hope to have on those around you?

### Day 275
How do you deal with distractions when you need to focus on important tasks?

### Day 276
What are your thoughts on the importance of self-discipline in achieving success?

### Day 277
How do you approach learning from people who are different from you?

### Day 278
What are your strategies for maintaining physical health amid a busy schedule?

### Day 279
How do you approach making amends in a relationship after a disagreement?

### Day 280
What are the most significant influences on your personal values?

## Day 281
How do you define personal success in relationships?

## Day 282
What steps do you take to ensure you are continuously learning and growing?

## Day 283
How do you navigate the challenges of maintaining your identity in a diverse social environment?

## Day 284
What are your favorite methods for relaxing and recharging after a long week?

## Day 285
How do you incorporate feedback from others to improve yourself?

## Day 286
How do you determine the reliability of news and information you encounter online?

## Day 287
What practices help you maintain a sense of calm and balance in stressful situations?

## Day 288
How do you handle the pressure to excel in all areas of your life, including academics, social circles, and personal interests?

## Day 289
What are your thoughts on the impact of volunteer work on personal and community development?

## Day 290
How do you deal with the challenge of juggling school responsibilities and personal life without feeling overwhelmed?

## Day 291
What strategies do you use to enhance your learning outside the classroom?

## Day 292
How do you approach dealing with criticism, whether constructive or not?

### Day 293
What steps do you take to foster a positive self-image when you feel down about yourself?

### Day 294
How do you nurture your relationships to ensure they are supportive and enriching?

### Day 295
What role does adventure or exploration play in your life?

### Day 296
How do you go about making a significant decision that affects both your current situation and future opportunities?

### Day 297
How do you advocate for your own needs in a respectful and effective manner?

### Day 298
What are your methods for dealing with procrastination, especially when facing tasks you don't enjoy?

### Day 299
How do you assess the impact of your actions on your peers and community?

### Day 300
What are your strategies for staying true to your values when faced with peer pressure?

## Day 301
How do you maintain enthusiasm for your long-term goals?

## Day 302
What are your thoughts on the importance of physical fitness to mental health?

## Day 303
How do you find balance between using technology for productivity and avoiding its distractions?

## Day 304
What are some ways you practice being kind to yourself during tough times?

## Day 305
How do you handle the fear of the unknown, especially when making plans for the future?

## Day 306
What are your strategies for effective communication in difficult conversations?

## Day 307
How do you maintain a sense of community while respecting individual differences?

## Day 308
What are your thoughts on the importance of lifelong learning?

## Day 309
How do you approach setting realistic goals and what steps do you take to achieve them?

## Day 310
How do you handle feeling out of place or different from others?

## Day 311
What methods do you use to assess your own progress in personal and academic achievements?

## Day 312
How do you deal with the disappointment of not meeting your own or others' expectations?

## Day 313
What are your views on the role of arts and culture in education?

## Day 314
How do you prepare yourself to take on leadership roles, whether in school or other areas?

## Day 315
How do you determine which aspects of your life need more attention or improvement?

## Day 316
What role does reflection play in your everyday decision-making?

### Day 317
How do you build and maintain trust in your personal and professional relationships?

### Day 318
What are your thoughts on the balance between giving and receiving in relationships?

### Day 319
How do you handle transitions, such as moving to a new school or city?

### Day 320
What are your strategies for coping with rejection, whether in friendships, academics, or other areas?

### Day 321
How do you engage with and contribute to your local or online community?

### Day 322
What personal traits have you worked on the most, and how have you developed them?

### Day 323
How do you ensure that you are respectful and inclusive in your interactions with others?

### Day 324
What are your thoughts on the importance of self-expression, and how do you express yourself?

### Day 325
How do you prioritize your mental health in your daily routine?

### Day 326
What are your strategies for overcoming barriers to your personal and academic goals?

### Day 327
How do you navigate the challenges of maintaining privacy and autonomy in your relationships?

### Day 328
What lessons have you learned from your travels or experiences in different cultures?

### Day 329
How do you foster a positive and supportive environment among your peers?

### Day 330
How do you approach learning about and engaging with global issues?

### Day 331
What are your favorite resources for personal development and learning?

### Day 332
How do you reconcile different aspects of your identity, such as your cultural background, interests, and personal beliefs?

### **Day 333**
What techniques do you find most effective for managing stress and maintaining a positive outlook?

### **Day 334**
How do you handle situations where you feel you're not being heard or understood?

### **Day 335**
What are your thoughts on the role of technology in shaping your future?

### **Day 336**
How do you approach balancing your personal goals with your responsibilities to others?

### Day 337
What are your strategies for handling stress during important life events, such as exams or family gatherings?

### Day 338
How do you identify and cultivate strengths you didn't know you had?

### Day 339
What role does community service play in your life, and why do you think it's important?

### Day 340
How do you approach conversations about your future plans with your parents or guardians?

### Day 341
What are some ways you seek to understand perspectives that are different from your own?

### Day 342
How do you manage your time effectively, especially when you feel overwhelmed by commitments?

### Day 343
What steps do you take to stay engaged and motivated in subjects that are not your strength?

### Day 344
How do you maintain your personal values when faced with societal pressures?

### Day 345
What are your methods for dealing with rejection or failure in a positive way?

### Day 346
How do you nurture your mental health and recognize signs that you might need to take a break?

### Day 347
What role do personal relationships play in your overall well-being?

### Day 348
How do you ensure that your use of social media is healthy and productive?

### Day 349
What are the most important factors that you consider when making new friendships?

### Day 350
How do you deal with peer pressure in social settings, especially when it involves alcohol or drugs?

### Day 351
What strategies do you use to maintain focus on long-term goals when immediate distractions are appealing?

### Day 352
How do you approach making amends in a relationship after a conflict?

## Day 353
What practices do you find helpful for enhancing your self-esteem?

## Day 354
How do you differentiate between constructive criticism and negative feedback?

## Day 355
What are your thoughts on the importance of role models in your life?

## Day 356
How do you deal with uncertainty about what you want to pursue in your future?

## Day 357
What are some ways you can actively support equality and inclusion in your community?

## Day 358
How do you find balance between striving for achievement and maintaining your health?

## Day 359
What are the benefits and challenges of working in team settings, and how do you navigate them?

## Day 360
How do you handle the pressures of societal expectations about your Appearance?

## Day 361

What methods do you use to approach learning and understanding complex topics?

## Day 362

How do you manage the stress of comparing yourself to others, especially in competitive environments?

## Day 363

What steps do you take to prepare for a significant transition, such as moving to college?

## Day 364

How do you assess the impact of your actions on your community and environment?

## Day 365
What personal achievements are you aiming for in the next year, and what plan have you devised to reach them?

## **<u>Share Your Experience</u>**

Thank you for choosing this book. We hope this has provided meaningful insights and fostered valuable conversations for you and your child.

Your feedback helps us improve and helps other parents and young readers discover this resource. Reviews increase the book's visibility, making it easier for those who might benefit from its content to find it.

If you found this book helpful, please take a moment to leave a review by scanning this QR code.

Your experience can inspire and guide others on their journey of self-discovery and growth. We appreciate your support. Thank you.

Devon & Mauricio

www.ingramcontent.com/pod-product-compliance
Lightning Source LLC
Chambersburg PA
CBHW081338120626

46546CB00011B/3394

9 781998 402465